BEHAVIOR CHANGE

a view from the inside out

D1456927

HANK FIEGER

Morgan James Publishing • New York

BEHAVIOR CHANGE

a view from the inside out

Library of Congress Control Number: 2008929646
ISBN: 978-1-60037-463-0   (Paperback)

PUBLISHED BY:
Morgan James Publishing, LLC
1225 Franklin Ave Suite 325
Garden City, NY 11530-1693
Toll Free 800-485-4943
www.MorganJamesPublishing.com

COVER DESIGN BY:
Bernard Rudden

INTERIOR DESIGN BY:
3 Dog Design
www.3dogdesign.net

In an effort to support local communities, raise awareness and funds, Morgan James Publishing donates one percent of all book sales for the life of each book to Habitat for Humanity. Get involved today, visit www.HelpHabitatForHumanity.org.

DISCLAIMER:

"What lies behind you and what lies in front of you, pales in comparison to what lies inside of you."

—Ralph Waldo Emerson

Dear Donna,

It's been a pleasure meeting you here in Spain.

All the best,

Henk

June '09
Barcelona

CONTENTS

DEDICATION

"At times our own light goes out and is rekindled by a spark from another person. Each of us has cause to think with deep gratitude of those who have lighted the flame within us."

—Albert Schweitzer

I dedicate this book:

To all of my teachers for what you have taught me.

To my peers for what I have learned from you and how you have helped me to develop my point of view.

To all of my clients and students—past and future—I hope to share profound simplicity with you.

To my parents for your love and support throughout my life.

To Prem Rawat (a.k.a. Maharaj) for what you have shown me to be the direct source of my life.

And, for Joannie
(1955-2007)

ACKNOWLEDGEMENTS

"If the only prayer you said in your whole life was, 'thank you,' that would suffice."

—Meister Eckhart

I AM INDEBTED AND GRATEFUL TO
Antioch University
The Ben-Chanochs
Dorothy Bolton
The Burgis
Catharine Clarke
Mitchell Ditkoff
Federico & Ida
The Fiegers
Tim Gallwey
David Hancock
The Henris
Rick Kahn
The Men's Group
My team at Morgan James Publishing
Ramon & Ana
Brian Riese
Gerhard Rumpff
David Vorzimer

ACCLAIM

What People are saying about *Behavior Change...A View From the Inside Out*

"A simple and straightforward guide to accessing your inner resources and making desired changes in your life. I heartily recommend it."

Tim Gallwey - Author of The Inner Game of Tennis and The Inner Game of Work

"This book is a wonderful reminder of all the resources already within us and provides a no nonsense "kick in the butt" to use those resources. The author draws on a depth of experience to show us in a clear and simple way to create shift in our lives."

Henry Kimsey-House - Author of Co-Active Coaching and co-founder of The Coaches Training Institute (CTI)

"Hank Fieger writes as well as he coaches -- helping others learn to modify deeply rooted behaviors that can affect performance and self potential. He understands the basics of human nature and what it takes to make the choice to change. Change is difficult but Hank's methods help identify limiting behaviors and discover replacements that can improve one's effectiveness."

Frank Kern - Senior Vice President, IBM

"Hank Fieger has distilled his many years of consulting and training experience to capture the essence of how people can take control of their life. I have used Behavior Change to help corporate managers and leaders achieve the results they desired in both their professional and personal lives. An essential read for anyone involved in training and development."

Alexander Grimshaw - CEO and Senior Partner,
PPS International Ltd.

"Keep this book handy as it will teach you how to "reprogram" yourself to become more effective no matter who you are or what you do. Not only will you notice the difference, so will everyone you deal with."

Bill Merrick - Ogilvy & Mather

"Behavior Change is a powerful tool for helping uncover the underlying assumptions that shape us as leaders. It's a must-read for anyone who wants to achieve more in their life, their work and the world."

Gloria Stinson - VP, Organizational Development
Adobe Systems Incorporated

"This wonderful example of how the author made changes in his own life, shows business leaders, teachers, coaches, therapists and individuals how to create lasting behavioral change. This handbook will guide the reader through the process of adapting, adjusting, and changing for the better."

Jacaranda Press - India

"Very focused, simple and touching. I really love your framework, for its seeming simplicity, yet touching on the much more fundamental underlying issues that govern our behaviors and ability/ willingness to change."

Sandra Visser - Essence Coaching

PREFACE

Within each and every person exists an internal structure or operating system. Most people who use a computer have no idea how its operating system works. In turn, most people have no clue how their own system works.

Computers come with a manual. People don't. Each individual carries deep beliefs about who he or she is—core values and attitudes toward life. Thoughts, feelings, choices, and behaviors emerge from within this essential inner place and set a life in motion as well as hold it in place. More often than not, when individuals want to change a behavior, they find its origins so deeply rooted to their identity that they cannot unravel the behavior from who they believe themselves to be and what they believe about life itself.

Behavior Change provides its readers with a perceptive understanding of what contributes to their existing behavior and how to approach, initiate, and implement real behavior change. Using a simple model, *Behavior Change* offers business leaders, teachers, therapists, coaches, actors—individuals from all walks of life—a working guide to help them modify, improve, and change their behavior. Changing behavior begins by knowing where specific behaviors originate. Simply becoming more aware allows individuals to make new choices that improve their behavior. Shift happens!

The essence of this work rests on the foundational principle that human behavior— visual (what we do), vocal (the volume, speed, and tone of our voice), and verbal (the actual words we say)—comes from a deep set of beliefs that firmly establishes values and attitudes, generates thoughts and feelings, presents choices, and ultimately creates behaviors. If individuals change behavior without exploring the roots of that behavior, when they experience stress or duress, the new behavior will likely revert to the old way.

This handbook intends to first demonstrate, with examples and clear logic, how thinking drives feelings, feelings drive behavior, and behavior drives results. Readers may then begin the process of adapting, adjusting, and changing their behavior. Others view, assess, judge, and compensate us based on our behavior—what they see us do, and what they hear us say. As the wise aphorism reminds: "Actions speak louder than words."

Embracing the belief that *effective behavior* resides within each individual, *Behavior Change* does not tell its readers what they need to do differently but rather illuminates the process of changing behavior based on these four fundamental principles of behavior change:

- **Awareness** and acceptance are the first steps to creating lasting change.

- **Understanding** what holds habitual behavior in place is key to doing things differently.

- **Improvement** means making a new choice and replacing old behavior patterns with more effective and productive ones.

- **Reinforcement** emphasizes that practice with feedback brings improvement.

Note: See *Chapter Two: Core Beliefs* for more detailed explanation of working with the four principles for creating lasting change.

Note: There are specific exercises at the end of some of the chapters where you will have the opportunity to put these four principles into practice. I highly recommend that you do the exercises before proceeding on in the book, as you will then develop a greater understanding of how to create lasting change in your life. There are blank note pages provided for you at the end of the book.

INTRODUCTION

"Life is what you make it, always has been, always will be."

—Grandma Moses

How many times in your life have you tried to change your behavior? Why is it so difficult to change? Has anyone ever asked you to change the way you do things? Have you ever come away from "personal growth" or leadership/management workshops, excited, full of realizations about your behavior and yet unable to make new behavior patterns stick? As a professional observer of human behavior, these are some of the important questions I've asked myself and others.

Although we may intellectually know that we could behave in a more effective way, we still have trouble changing. Why are we such "creatures of habit"? Over my 30 years as a professional, coaching and training people to change their behavior, I know all too well myself and in my experience with others, how difficult it is to change behavior.

THE SYSTEM, THE PROGRAM, AND THE PROGRAMMER

Thinking about the variety of psychological and philosophical systems that exist, I am struck by how many intelligent individuals—from scientists to theoreticians—have attempted to understand how we function as human beings. Quite simply, I believe that our internal operating system, our internal structure, contributes to how we think, speak, and behave, in the same way that an operating system contributes to how a computer functions.

Our core beliefs, whether originating with us at birth or learned as a child, make our individual "programs" unique. Carl G. Jung, the great Swiss psychologist, believed that we come into this life with a predisposition. On the other hand, Aristotle said that "we are like a clean tablet on which nothing is written." Whether based on nature or nurture, our beliefs, values, attitude, thoughts, feelings, and choices affect our behaviors. And, therefore, in order to make changes within our internal "program," we must take responsibility as our own "programmer."

As we continuously make choices—consciously, subconsciously, and unconsciously—our internal programming contributes to the outcomes of our lives. Each of us sits at the helm of our own journey. We drive and steer our lives in the direction that we want to go. We can affect changes at all levels of our being, if we choose to do so. There is no need to experience ourselves as victims.

How do we set these changes in motion? By waking up and becoming aware of the program that drives our life. With that awareness, we can look at the beliefs, thoughts, and actions that are operating in our lives. If we want to change them, we must understand what keeps them in place. We must make new choices. We can choose to change a belief, a thought pattern, or a behavior in order to change the internal program that can so deeply contribute to the reality of our lives.

PERFORMANCE = POTENTIAL − SELF-INTERFERENCE

In 1976 I went to work for Timothy Gallwey, author of *The Inner Game of Tennis*. Tim taught me how to coach individuals "from the inside out" by introducing me to a very simple approach that he called the "Art of Relaxed Concentration." This approach was based on a profoundly uncomplicated formula: *Performance = Potential − Self Interference*. Through a series of exercises and self-awareness, students learned how to get out of their own way.

Our own unique potential lives within each of us, waiting, even longing, to be fulfilled. We don't need to add anything. In fact, learning, performing, and behaving to our fullest potential depends upon our willingness to identify and minimize our self-interference. As you likely realize, this is not a new concept. Knowledge exists within us, around us, in front of us, and behind us. My experience tells me that there's nothing new being taught; instead we're called to rediscover what we already know. The first step toward change calls for nonjudgmental awareness of what exists—then shift can happen.

Self-awareness allows us to witness how we interfere with our potential and how such interference affects our behavior. Having wondered and explored for many years where our behavior originates, why we behave the way we do—both professionally and personally—I've come to understand that an internal process occurs prior to our behavior. We subconsciously listen to our thoughts and feelings and often act automatically rather than consciously hearing what they really say. Through self-awareness, we may learn how we truly think and feel and respond from that place rather than reacting habitually and therefore interfering with our inner knowing.

Still, where do our thoughts and feelings come from? Why do we look at life as we do? What's really important to us in our life right now? Who do we believe we are, and how do we see the world we live in? *Behavior Change* intends to guide you toward the answers to these and other underlying questions that have until now kept you running in place rather than making the changes that match your potential.

The first sentence in Scott Peck's powerful book, *The Road Less Traveled* begins, "Life is difficult." This statement has stayed with me over the years, and I've often asked myself, "Why is life so difficult for so many of us?" After much soul-searching, study, and bringing my awareness to my daily interactions with people, I've come to believe that life is difficult if we make it so. Life is _____. (You fill in the blank.) It appears that we struggle with life not because we're lacking potential but because we're unaware.

I want to heighten your awareness of that part of you that came built in, that part of you that reflects who you truly are and that deeply affects your daily life. We don't arrive ill-equipped into this life. In fact, we come fully equipped. It's our self-interference that makes life difficult.

We're constantly making choices and creating behaviors that have consequences or trade-offs. How conscious are you of this ongoing process? By heightening your awareness, you can deepen your understanding of why you do what you do, and how your core beliefs are ultimately expressed in your behavior. Plus, this handbook will introduce you to tools that can assist you in discovering who you are and how you function.

Behavior Change intends to simplify your learning process. We all can rediscover how to learn naturally no matter what we want to learn, change, or accept. We unconsciously used the same natural process as children when we learned how to walk and to talk—it's integral to the whole human package. In a world of technical sophistication and an abundance of psychological and self-help books, we tend to complicate simple processes, losing touch with our most intrinsic gifts. We eagerly want to learn "how to be more ourselves" instead of simply being who we already are.

A Japanese proverb underscores this idea: "Tension is who we think we should be….Relaxation is who we are." And, in Pema Chodron's wonderful book, *The Wisdom of No Escape*, she considers "self-improvement" an aggressive act towards oneself, asserting that our potential needs no self-improvement. She instead suggests that we need more self-acceptance.

GROUND RULES

Before we begin, let's establish some ground rules. As you prepare to examine your behavior using this book's simple approach, first try to suspend your judgment for now and put aside "good and bad" and "right and wrong." Such terms polarize our thinking and impede the receptivity that learning requires. We all judge; it's the nature of our rational minds. But rather than harshly judging your beliefs, feelings, choices, and behaviors as "good or bad," see them instead as "effective or less effective." This approach allows you to shift and change those patterns that no longer serve you.

PRESENCE

If the first step to changing your behavior is self-awareness, the first step to self-awareness is being present in each given moment. And, rediscovering your innate potential, as shared within *Behavior Change*, asks for your full presence while reading this handbook. Life happens in the present moment. The past is history—a memory that we can learn from. The future remains only a vision until we reach it. The desire to shift certain behaviors takes place now, here, in the present moment. Your awareness of the core beliefs, values, or attitudes that keep those habitual behavior patterns static also happens in the present moment.

Presence means to fully engage yourself in the present moment. It informs your self-awareness and therefore your intentions as well as your ability to focus your attention.

INTENTION AND ATTENTION

Intention and attention hold the keys to our learning process.

Intention shapes our destiny. Surely you have heard "Be careful what you wish for, you might just get it." Our intention sets our goals in motion. What do you want to accomplish? What is your desired outcome? In *The Seven Habits of Highly Effective People*, Stephen Covey suggests that we "Begin with the end in mind". I like to say, "Purpose before action" as a guide for clarifying our intention.

Attention tells you where you are. In other words, as author and professor of medicine, Jon Kabat-Zinn, has said, "Wherever you go, there you are". If you place your attention in the past, then you're in the past; if you focus on the future, then that's where you'll find yourself. Likewise, if your attention is in the present, then you're here now. Sound like a cliché? Even though we hear this a lot these days, it's no less true.

As you work through the chapters ahead, stay in close touch with your intention and where you're focusing your attention.

IMAGINATION, DESIRE, AND TRUST

To review: our internal core beliefs continually affect our experiences. Your belief about who you are and what you value; your attitude, thoughts, or feelings about what and why you're doing what you're doing; your choices about moment-to-moment decisions—all point to how you actually behave.

In turn, your **imagination** reflects how you would like yourself to be; your **desire** longs to make that happen, and your **trust** allows you to let it happen. By understanding how we internally function and using the tools of imagination, desire, and trust, we contribute to creating our own reality. As adults, we choose not to be victims *of* life but rather to co-create *with* life.

RESPONSIBILITY AND ACCOUNTABILITY

Recently, a friend's comments reminded me how sometimes we not only avoid taking responsibility for our actions but also the consequences of those actions. In response to a recent fortunate situation, the friend responded with statements such as: "The universe brought this to me" and "Isn't the universe amazing how it put me in this situation?" Though said in a positive way, these comments struck me as "victim" consciousness. There seems little question that greater life forces operate independently from us and often present us with opportunities for growth. However, we become empowered when we learn to take responsibility for our behavior, to own the impact of our choices on our lives and on the lives of others. Our presence and self-awareness prepare us to make this effort.

A client of mine once told me that the definition of luck is "when preparation meets opportunity." Sometimes the opportunity presents itself, but we aren't prepared for it. Other times we are prepared and nothing seems to happen; no opportunity knocks. When the two come together, however, we might say that we were "in the right place at the right time," or we were "lucky". To co-create our reality, we must meet each moment prepared and ready to take responsibility with accountability for the outcome.

In other words, you can only manage your half of any relationship. The question becomes: "How effectively are you managing your half?" Whether in relationship with another person or with the greater life forces, the key is to focus on how we are contributing to the results we are experiencing. This dynamic asks us to take responsibility and to be accountable for our part in those results. We constantly contribute to our reality. By examining our internal structure and how we operate, we glimpse the nature of our partnership with life. As we take the appropriate responsibility for our lives, we may also surrender to the ease that lies within any difficult moment.

* * *

In an effort to ground the work introduced here by reflecting upon my personal experience, and to encourage you, the reader, to do the same, I want to share a bit of my personal story.

My background as a coach, consultant, and trainer in interpersonal communication and personal development began with my parents. As a young boy, I realized very quickly that in order to connect with my mother, I must communicate with her. Though emotionally reserved and not very physically demonstrative, she was very communicative and available to talk and to listen about many subjects. I would come home from school, sit in the kitchen or in my parents' bedroom, and listen to her talk about her day; then I would tell her about mine. In this way I learned about the importance of communication very early in my life. More of a people person, my dad was physically and emotionally demonstrative but not as talkative as my mother, so each shared with me a different communication style.

I grew up in the 1950s in the suburbs of New York City. My childhood wasn't difficult (or very memorable), and my parents provided security and comfort for the family. In 1960 when the country elected John F. Kennedy as President of the United States, I vividly remember the excitement around his election in my home and school. Then on November 22, 1963, I remember walking down the hallway in school when a friend passed me and exclaimed, "Hey, the President has been shot!" When I entered my history class I saw my teacher (who was also one of my football coaches) sitting at his desk and crying. I was devastated; one of my heroes was dead. When the same thing happened in 1968 to Martin Luther King and then to Robert Kennedy, I began to question everything.

I finished high school and went on to college, still questioning everything. (In the late sixties, many of us questioned everything.) I graduated in 1969 and had the good fortune to go to Woodstock, the music festival that defined my generation. From there, I was drafted into the U. S. Army to go to Vietnam but managed to fail my physical. I then got a Eurail pass, a backpack, and an open, round-trip ticket to Europe. I traveled and visited 18 countries in 10 months, and my eyes opened to how other people lived around the world. I knew then that I wanted to continue to travel the world.

When I came back to the States, for a short while I worked in Manhattan before moving to Berkeley, California in 1970 to join in the cultural revolution happening there. After a few years, I moved to Chico, a university town three hours north of San Francisco. I bought some land; opened a small business in the town; studied Buckminster Fuller; built a geodesic dome with the help of friends; lived in an Indian teepee with my brother, James; tended an organic garden, and lived out my hippie fantasies. In the midst of all of this, my brother and I were introduced to a teacher from India who offered a technique of meditation called Self-Knowledge. His name was Prem Rawat (a.k.a. Maharaji).

On Easter Sunday 1976, my business, along with six others, burned down. Rather than rebuilding it, I decided to move to Los Angeles to connect with a larger community of meditators and experience life in a big city. There I met Timothy Gallwey, the author of *The Inner Game of Tennis*, and he asked me to be part of his company, The Inner Game. After working with Tim for many years, I went back to graduate school at Antioch University to study psychology. When finished, I went to work with Ridge Associates where I learned the art of training and leading others in Interpersonal Communication Skills. After helping Ridge to build their West Coast network of trainers, in 1990 I left them to become an external trainer for Apple Computer. Since then I've continued my work with IBM, Adobe, Ogilvy and Mather, and other companies as a coach, consultant, and trainer in interpersonal communication and personal development.

In 2007, I lost my younger sister, Joannie, to lung cancer. Her passing has deeply affected me and taught me about the preciousness of this life.

"The way of the masters was to find their own way."

—Zen proverb

CHAPTER 1

Our Internal Operating System

(How We Contribute to Our Own Reality)

"Human beings are the only species that have the ability to get in the way of their own growth."

—Fritz Perls

We all encounter people who want us to change our behavior, from our early childhood to as recently as today. Parents, teachers, managers, priests, rabbis, ministers, counselors, therapists, coaches, husbands, wives, girlfriends, boyfriends, society—all request us to change. Sometimes we ourselves want to change. But how do we go about it? It's ironic that we're never taught *how* to change our behavior.

It has been said that sometimes people only change when the pain of not changing becomes greater than the pain of changing. I propose that by understanding *how we function* as human beings we can *choose* to change without waiting for pain to motivate us.

Facilitating effective communication skills, specifically interpersonal "people skills" for mid- and upper-management, continues to challenge and teach me lessons about how and why people behave the way they do. Many of my clients work in the information technology industry, such as IBM, Apple Computer, Microsoft, Adobe, Cisco, and

Sybase. I have observed that many engineers and technically trained individuals usually don't have very strong interpersonal skills; it's typically not their strength.

When we consider "people skills," we simply believe that an individual either has them or they don't. Much of my work involves helping others through the process of behavior change, whether it's learning to improve their interpersonal skills or simply changing the way they do things. My experience has shown me that changing behavior can be learned at any age.

When organizations conduct employee surveys, many responders may say, "Management doesn't listen to us," prompting human resources managers to hire trainers, consultants, or coaches like myself to help their managers become better listeners. Everyone in an eight- or even four-hour class of "Active Listening Skills" can learn the technique. Yet I found that for some reason only a small percentage of such managers actually change their behavior when they arrive back on the job. A few clearly respond to the new skill and integrate and use it in their work process. Some experiment with it, but when they encounter a difficult situation, they tend to discard the new skill altogether. Others never intend to use it, as they don't believe it will make a difference. They don't seem to value listening in general, or what his or her employees have to say.

Why do those who choose to use the new skills, when put under stress or duress, revert back to their old habits? In the mid-'80s, my initial concern over this and other such questions encouraged me to examine my role and effectiveness as a trainer, consultant, and coach and to explore how much behavior change actually takes place. I began looking for the key, tool, insight, or "ah ha!" that enables people to effectively let go of an old habit and completely integrate a new behavior.

I intuitively found that my behavior originated from an internal structure or process inherent to the human being, and I believed it was the same for others. How odd, I thought, that so many of us don't know who we are and live a perpetual quest to "know thyself," as Socrates said. I said, "Isn't it our birthright to know who we are and why we are here?"

I call this internal structure within each human being: Our Internal Operating System. Bill Gates has recently referred to the Digital Nervous System in his book, *Business @ The Speed of Thought*. He asserts that an organization, like a computer, can learn from the human to become even more effective. On the other hand, I am fascinated by what human beings can learn from the computer to become more effective people.

> *"We don't see things as they are,*
> *we see them as we are."*

> **—Anais Nin**

This simple flow diagram illustrates how our internal operating system works:

OUR INTERNAL OPERATING SYSTEM
(How we contribute to our own reality)

CORE BELIEFS
↓
VALUES
↓
ATTITUDE
↓
THOUGHTS AND FEELINGS
↓
CHOICES
↓
BEHAVIORS

Our deep set of **core beliefs**, those ideas we believe to be true about our-selves and the world in which we live, contribute to the formation of our values. Our **values**, those principles that carry great importance for us, inform our attitude. Our **attitude** reflects the set of lenses through which we see the world around us. Our core beliefs, values, and attitude exist deep within us, and because they establish the foundation for who we are and how we see the world, we seldom reconsider them. Only when a situation or person questions our values, or we're asked to do something that compromises one of our principles, do we reflect upon what's truly important to us. Such instances are called "value dilemmas".

Otherwise most of us assume that we operate the way we do because "that's who we are."

Most of us are in touch with ourselves through our **thoughts and feelings**. We make **choices** based on what we think and how we feel. We listen to our head through our logic and to our heart through our emotions. Our choices lead to decisions and thus contribute to our **behaviors**.

Shakti Gawain first introduced me to the concept of "Be, Do, Have" in her book *Creative Visualization*. Most of us live our lives from a "Have, Do, Be" approach. For example, first we must get the promotion, then we can behave like a VP so we will be successful. Our Internal Operating System embraces the "Be, Do, Have" approach. For example, by redefining our core beliefs we can begin to experience ourselves as successful, loving, and deserving which will in turn affect our attitude so that we can begin making choices and behaving like successful, loving, deserving people. Such behavior gives us what successful, loving, and deserving people receive. We don't need to have something to believe that we deserve it. By establishing that belief, we can then choose to act "as if" we already *have* it. Ironically, behaving "as if" manifests what we believe that we deserve; you step into what you've already structured. By simply changing what you believe, it can become your reality. Shift happens!

The succeeding six chapters explain in detail the progression outlined above and invite you to reflect upon each segment of your internal operating system to reveal clearly how you and your operating system work. You will find some exercises in many of the chapters to help you reflect upon the beliefs, values, and thoughts and feelings that are now operating within you. Whether you choose to read this handbook, one chapter a day, or one chapter a week, or read it straight through, it is highly recommended that you do the exercises before proceeding on to the following chapters. By doing so, you will gain greater awareness and will find it easier to make conscious choices as you read through the book. With that awareness and understanding, hopefully you will feel well equipped to change those behaviors that you find to be less effective and to accept and strengthen those that serve you well.

If ya always do whatcha always done, then yer always gonna get whatcha always got.

—Old Southern proverb

CHAPTER 2

CORE BELIEFS

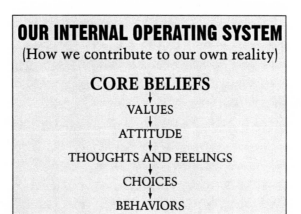

OUR INTERNAL OPERATING SYSTEM
(How we contribute to our own reality)

CORE BELIEFS
↓
VALUES
↓
ATTITUDE
↓
THOUGHTS AND FEELINGS
↓
CHOICES
↓
BEHAVIORS

"If I have the belief that I can do it, I shall surely acquire the capacity to do it even if I may not have it at the beginning."

—Mahatma Gandhi

As established in Chapter One, deep within us exists a set of core beliefs—those ideas that we believe about ourselves and the world we live in. Whether or not they are true is irrelevant; if we believe them, they become true for us and ultimately contribute to our behavior. For example, if I believe that the world is a friendly place, I behave in an open, curious, trusting, adventurous, and risk-taking manner. With this belief firmly in place, I tend to attract open, curious, friendly, adventurous, risk-taking people, and this supports my belief. "See," I might say, "the world is a friendly place; I make friends everywhere." If instead I believe that the world is a dangerous place, I am more likely to behave in a more closed, cautious, suspicious, mistrusting, and risk-averse manner. And, with this firm belief, guess what I attract? Predators! Walk down the street in any major city in the world appearing defensive and cautious and notice who and what you attract. "See," you will likely say, "the world is a dangerous place; you must always be very careful."

When do we form these core beliefs and what instigates them? And how does our behavior create self-fulfilling prophecies? Core beliefs form at different times in our life. Some develop early in childhood, and by six, seven, or eight years old, they strongly affect our behavior. As we approach adolescence and adulthood, we may reinforce childhood core beliefs and/or form new ones based on our more recent life experiences.

Recently, I conducted a team-building session in Europe for a very large multinational software company, and one of the participants asked, "Can I change my core beliefs, or am I just hard-wired that way?" This insightful question led me to reflect on my own experience with core beliefs. I've found that we can change at that deep level, but it requires both self-awareness and reinforcement.

The following example from my own life illustrates how a core belief develops as well as how to change it. (Using this belief, I demonstrate throughout the book how it affected my internal operating system and contributed to the way I live my life.)

When I was a boy of eight growing up on Long Island, New York, I took my first mathematics test in third grade.

I received a grade of 98% out of 100% on my test. Very excited to share the news with my mother, I remember sitting in class somewhat distracted, watching the clock, and waiting until finally three o'clock came. When the final bell rang, I ran the entire way home from school and burst into my house exclaiming, "Mom, Mom, Mom!"

My mother, who had been tending to my baby sister, came into the kitchen and asked, "What's the matter, son?"

"I got a 98 on my math test. Isn't that great?" I replied.

My mother looked at me calmly and asked, "Why didn't you get a 100?"

My mother loved me then, and she still loves me now. She loves her family very much. She meant no harm. She only wanted the best for her children. She may have even said, "That's good. Why didn't you get a 100?" However, that very excited little eight-year-old boy interpreted the message as, "Not quite good enough." Walking away deflated, I took her comment and personalized it further to mean "I'm not quite good enough." I then formed a deep-seated belief that "I am not enough." For the next ten years, I attempted to become enough. I tried earnestly to fill my room with trophies, honors, awards, plaques, and so on. I went out for everything: sports, theater, school politics, and so on. I became an overachiever. I needed one thing: for a very specific someone, my Mom, to tell me that I was enough—just the way I was. I learned how to perform for love and took this core belief and its subsequent attitude into the rest of my life.

Looking back, I realize that I didn't much enjoy all of my achieving. In fact attempting to be a perfect kid became quite stressful, leading to my struggle with asthma for the first eleven years of my life and developing a hiatal hernia by the time I was twenty. When I was in the hospital for the hiatal hernia, the doctors—though not very psychologically oriented—told me that I needed to change my life, or I would kill myself from the inside.

Ironically, after I graduated from college and entered the business world, and had just finished my first project, my boss said, "Great job." Like winning awards and plaques before, I received the acknowledgment that I'd so desperately wanted. But once again, I couldn't let it in. A small, all-too-familiar voice inside my head responded silently, "But I could have done even better. He doesn't know what I left out." I had absorbed my mother's criticism from long ago and had become my own "critical parent."

Until a few years ago, I lived my life with the belief that "I am not enough," watching my behavior vacillate between trying to be the best and not wanting to try at all. Even though I was successful as a teacher/coach/trainer/consultant, no matter how well I did; no matter how much my clients liked my work; and no matter how much my parents, lovers, family, and friends loved me, I was never satisfied with myself. After practicing meditation for many years, studying psychology, and reading many insightful books by great teachers, I finally came to realize that only changing my deepest beliefs could change this pattern. I knew I must shift my thinking in order to bring personal satisfaction into my life. I decided to experiment with altering my experience—to see what life would be like if I changed a core belief. For one week, I committed to a new core belief: "I am enough." Immediately the small voice inside my head resisted and said, "You will not be very productive." It knew what drove my productivity. Nevertheless, I persevered, trying the new belief on for size. It became my focus in everything I did. I would begin each morning writing in a journal to reinforce this new belief. I would write myself notes and leave them around the house. I would say it out loud, when I was alone. To my surprise, at the end of the week I noticed that I had actually been more effective and productive than ever before. I realized that prior to that week, and for as long as I could remember, I performed to win approval: "Do you love me now?" "Am I good enough now?" I always believed that I was a very giving person. It was only after this short experiment, that I came to understand how so much of my behavior was really about my need to get. The act of giving was my attempt to get something back in return. I performed for love.

My short experiment proved to me that even long-held core beliefs could be changed. My new belief created new behavior supported by my deep need to give. I uncovered a real meaning for my existence—the great satisfaction of truly giving. I learned that discipline was required in order to train my self in new ways of thinking and being.

I also discovered many other core beliefs that had operated within me, such as, "I can add value to this life" and "I can make a difference." Reflecting upon these other core beliefs, I discovered that they also came from my parents. I remember them saying, "Son, you can do anything you put your heart and mind to," and "You can make a difference in people's lives." When I pointed out injustices that I saw when young, my mother wisely advised me, "Don't just complain about it; do something to change it." Our more "critical" beliefs tend to overshadow the more "supportive" beliefs. Some examples of critical beliefs are "not good enough," "not loveable," "not as smart as others," "can't compete with others," "I don't add any value." Some of the more supportive beliefs are "I can make a difference," "I'm very capable," "I'm loveable," "I have a unique gift to give to the world," "I have value." When we shift the "critical" beliefs, our newfound awareness opens us to discover and reap the benefits of the "supportive" beliefs. (It is important to note that usually more than one belief operates within us at a given time.)

Becoming aware of the beliefs that operate within us, understanding what keeps them in place, making a different choice, and reinforcing a new belief, all allow us to create lasting change.

The exercise below offers an introduction to working with your core beliefs, followed by a process to help you change, or at least modify, a belief or any aspect of your life that you think needs improvement.

EXERCISE: IDENTIFY YOUR CORE BELIEFS

Use this simple but revealing exercise to introduce yourself to a group, to another person, or perhaps to yourself—and to learn about your core beliefs.

1. Take ten minutes in silence and identify the most important people, places, and events that have contributed to who you are right now at this moment in your life.

2. Next, take five minutes to share this information, out loud, with a group or another person. It's your life story. It's not necessary to use the entire five minutes, but don't exceed the five-minute limit. The time constraint encourages you to spontaneously choose these key people, places, and events from a place of inner knowing rather than to deliberate and analyze who and/or what has greatly influenced who you are and how you live. If you prefer to work with this exercise privately, you can either write down what you would say or speak it into a tape recorder. In either case,

make sure to limit yourself to only five minutes. (See my own story on pages xxvi-xxix, that told of those important people, places, and events that contributed to who I am today.)

3. Now notice what you chose to share with the group or other person, or what you chose to focus on privately.

4. Take some time and identify the strong beliefs that you hold true for yourself and the world you live in.

    The key is to view them without judgment. They are your beliefs; they are not good or bad. The question to ask yourself is: *How does this belief effectively or ineffectively serve my life right now?* Certain beliefs may have served you well at times in your life but no longer.

5. Choose one of the beliefs that is no longer serving you and can imagine changing it. Experiment for a week with changing this belief and observe how this change affects your attitude and ultimately your behavior. Ask yourself, how did this belief serve you in the past? What was the payoff? What was the cost? What did you get by having this belief? What did you lose by having this belief?

CREATING LASTING CHANGE

As introduced in the preface, the process for creating lasting change consists of these four principles:

1. **Awareness**: Recognizing the limiting belief that affects you

2. **Understanding**: Discovering what keeps the belief in place

3. **Improvement**: Replacing the belief with one that's more supportive

4. **Reinforcement**: Consciously practicing the new belief

Whether you want to change your core beliefs, your inner voice, your golf swing, or the way you manage your time and activities in the office, these principles offer you the steps necessary to create change that becomes your new way of behaving.

AWARENESS

If you're not aware of it, you can't change it. First, you must identify the belief, behavior, or habit that you want to change, modify, or shift. Self-awareness is half of the work; it turns on the light, revealing what's actually going on. Feedback— whether from others or from the results of your actions or thoughts—may jolt you awake, but conscious awareness requires that you pay attention to your beliefs and accept that they exist, especially if you want to change them. As a teacher of mine once said, "You can't get out of jail if you don't even know you're in there." You must become aware of your limitations in order to transcend them.

UNDERSTANDING

Once you've identified the belief or behavior that you want to change, it's important to understand where it originated or what provoked it. Discovering these underpinnings loosens its grip. You're keeping it in place, consciously or unconsciously, because it serves you in some way. There's a payoff. Until you accept this responsibility and understand what's behind the belief or behavior, you can't detach from it or choose a new behavior with which to replace it. Ask yourself these questions: Where does this belief come from? How is it affecting my behavior? What is it giving me? What is the payoff for continuing to do it the same way over and over again? How is it limiting me?"

IMPROVEMENT

Now that you are aware of what it is that you want to change and you know what is keeping it in place, you've taken ownership of it. This is key, as you need to realize that it belongs to you, for better or worse. You most likely put it there, as it served you at some point in your life. If you determine that it no longer serves you, and, in fact, may be hindering or holding you back from what you really want in your life, then you can make a different choice and change it.

Don't struggle with trying to break a "bad" habit or willfully get rid of it. This negative attention actually keeps it in place. You give it life. Instead, ask yourself: "Is this behavior effective?" or "Is this habit helping me?" And if your answer is "not really," you can choose to replace it, or improve it. If this new way of doing or being serves you better, if it's more effective, then the old behavior will simply fall away.

For example, as a child progresses from crawling to walking, first he crawls for some time. He then will likely experiment with standing by holding on to things. Then one day he takes his first steps, perhaps taking a step or two before falling. Then the child gets up, and the process continues. Soon after those first tentative steps, typically within a week, he walks across the room. Rarely does a child go back to crawling, because walking is a much more effective way of getting around. This dynamic and practical method of learning happens naturally rather than cognitively and continues to operate within us as adults.

REINFORCEMENT

To create a new outcome, you must support the new belief or behavior with practice, practice, and more practice. Practice doesn't make perfect. Practice makes habits. Practice makes permanent. Practice creates grooves. Perfection—that's a spiritual discussion.

Every time I attempt to do something perfectly, I come up short. It's a setup for disappointment. Every time I attempt to improve on what I'm doing, I come away more satisfied.

Practice with feedback brings improvement. Just as a parent reinforces a child with smiles, applause, and positive comments, so our new behavior needs reinforcement. For example, if I want to change my communication skills, I must consciously practice with the people in my life. By noticing the way they react to my new skills, how it feels to use the new skills, and by asking them for feedback, I reinforce the new results while seeding lasting change.

Feedback is essential at the beginning of the process in order to heighten our awareness and also at the end of the process to reinforce our new way of doing and being. When we experience our new belief or behavior as more effective, more pleasurable, and more desirable, then the new behavior will become part of us.

"Belief without the experience is a lie.
The 'truth' is so damn believable, that we would rather believe it
rather than experience it."

—Anonymous

CHAPTER 3

VALUES

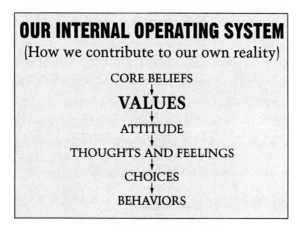

OUR INTERNAL OPERATING SYSTEM
(How we contribute to our own reality)

CORE BELIEFS
↓
VALUES
↓
ATTITUDE
↓
THOUGHTS AND FEELINGS
↓
CHOICES
↓
BEHAVIORS

*"Open your arms to change,
but don't let go of your values."*

—The Dalai Lama

What's most important to you in your life right now?

What you consider most important is what you most value. My very simple understanding of the existentialist view of life is that we exist; then we give value to our existence. I am here, breathing, existing. What gives meaning to my life is the meaning that I give to it. It's really that simple. We spend so much time comparing and competing while giving very little time, if any, to reflecting upon what we value during each stage of our lives. When we compete and compare, we enter a "less than/ more than" mentality that perpetuates judgment.

In *Man's Search for Meaning,* Victor Frankl tells his story of surviving a Nazi concentration camp. The story implies that those who valued the things taken away from them had difficulty surviving. While those, like Frankl, who gave meaning to their simple existence, endured. When faced with the finality of death, he and others had to look at what they valued in their lives. Sometimes it is only when we are faced with difficult decisions or life threatening situations that we stop to consider what is of real importance.

Individual values affect many levels of our behavior— both at work and in our personal lives. Values affect:

- Our initiative and dedication to achieve,

- Our efficiency and standards,

- Our attention to intra- and interpersonal connection,

- Our patience and perseverance with mundane activities,

- Our tendency to question, and

- Our service for the common good rather than self-satis-faction.

Our core beliefs profoundly impact our values. Years ago, when I completed a values review and clarification exercise with the belief, "I am not enough," originating from the childhood experience shared in Chapter Two, I clarified my values as: excellence, productivity, success, and competition. Changing that belief to "I am enough," my values have since changed to: integrity, peace of mind, balance, love, helping others, self-expression, and relationships. Excellence remains valuable to me, but its place of importance in my life has declined significantly.

A colleague recently shared this wonderful and clever example of the important role that values play in our lives:

- *To realize the value of ONE YEAR, ask a student who has failed his exam.*

- *To realize the value of ONE MONTH, ask a mother of a premature baby.*

- *To realize the value of ONE WEEK, ask an editor of a weekly newspaper.*

- *To realize the value of ONE DAY, ask a daily wage laborer who has kids to feed.*

- *To realize the value of ONE HOUR, ask the lovers who are waiting to meet.*

- *To realize the value of ONE MINUTE, ask a person who has missed the train.*

- *To realize the value of ONE SECOND ask the person who has survived an accident.*

- *To realize the value of ONE MILLISECOND ask the person who has won a silver medal in the Olympics.*

These definitions clarify the meaning of values:

- A value expresses a quality by which an individual sets a desirable standard for guiding decisions and actions.

- A value conveys a belief in a specific mode of conduct or behavior personally and socially more acceptable or preferable to another.

Usually when we meet new people we ask them what they do rather than who they are. The response typically identifies their profession, money, position, diplomas, achievements, and tangible assets. But we are truly more than our possessions and our achievements. When we understand what we value and revere, it becomes natural to behave in keeping with who we are. When we achieve clarity and understanding about what fuels our actions, we ensure that the end result supports and creates what we want and need.

EXERCISE: VALUES REVIEW AND CLARIFICATION

This exercise asks you to choose those values that you feel are most important to you. You will then review the list and narrow your choices to your ten primary values.

Don't over-think or spend too much time analyzing each word; simply respond to the list and remain open to your discoveries.

OBJECTIVES • To help you define and clarify those values that are most important to you in your life.

DIRECTIONS • Using the responses below, on the following pages indicate how frequently you consider each of the listed values:

O Often valued
S Sometimes valued
R Rarely valued

• If you want to add more values, use the blanks at the end of the lists.

VALUES CHECKLIST

___ Gathering new knowledge
___ Intellectual challenge
___ Problem solving
___ Hands-on work
___ Intellectual status
___ Simplicity
___ Making decisions
___ Contact with others
___ High earnings
___ Power and authority
___ Persuading
___ Leading others
___ Taking risks
___ Fast pace
___ Structure
___ Dependability
___ Order
___ Creativity
___ Aesthetics
___ Independence
___ Recognition
___ Management
___ Learning
___ Honesty
___ Success
___ Support
___ Balance

___ Competence
___ Competition
___ Physical challenge
___ Trust
___ Working with tools
___ Working outdoors
___ Health and fitness
___ Practicality
___ Adventure
___ Helping others
___ Community
___ Friendship
___ Affiliation
___ Stability
___ Discipline
___ Security
___ Variety
___ Self-expression
___ Originality
___ Freedom
___ Advancement
___ Family
___ Financial independence
___ Respect
___ Credibility
___ Dedication
___ Excellence

___ Harmony	___ Fun
___ Understanding	___ Cooperation
___ Reliability	___ Consistency
___ Commitment	___ Peace of Mind
___ Compassion	___ Consciousness
___ Responsiveness	___ Persistence
___ Generosity	___ Forgiveness
___ Achievement	___ Appreciation
___ Loyalty	___ Innovation
___ Communication	___ Accountability
___ Courage	___ Relationships
___ Free thinking	___ Spirituality
___ Willingness	___ Acceptance
___ Love	___ Efficiency
___ Enthusiasm	___ Preparation and planning
___ Patience	___ Integrity
___	___

DIRECTIONS • Review the list and from those values you've marked as "often," narrow your choices to your ten most important values.

• Notice that some of the words may have similar meaning to you, so don't choose two that are nearly the same.

• If you were asked to choose your top three values, which ones would you choose and in what order would you list them?

• Answer the following questions for each of your top three values.

VALUE #1 _____

1. How do I define this value? What does it mean to me personally?

2. How would my life be different if I demonstrated more of this value?

3. What could I do to have more of this value in my life?

Remember to answer these questions for your Value #2 and Value #3.

As you now study your choices, think back to your core beliefs and observe how they have manifested in those values most important to your life. This reflects who you believe yourself to be and how you experience the world in which you live. Are you beginning to see the patterns?

Again, when we understand what we value and revere, it becomes natural to behave in keeping with who we are. In other words, the means justify and support the end, and we live in alignment with our values and beliefs. When we seek the clarity and understanding of what drives our actions, we guarantee that our actions will create and support what we want and need.

"Values are the precious reminders that individuals obey to bring order and meaning into their personal lives."

—James Michener

CHAPTER 4

ATTITUDE

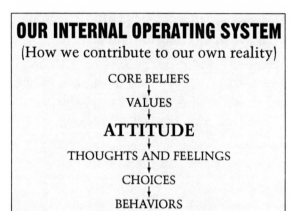

OUR INTERNAL OPERATING SYSTEM
(How we contribute to our own reality)

CORE BELIEFS
↓
VALUES
↓
ATTITUDE
↓
THOUGHTS AND FEELINGS
↓
CHOICES
↓
BEHAVIORS

"If the doors of perception were cleansed, everything would appear as it truly is...infinite."

—William Blake

Others do not easily see our core beliefs and values, which exist at a very deep level of our being. Unless you tell me what yours are, I can only guess or surmise who you believe yourself to be and what you consider important. However, your attitude can begin to reveal how your core beliefs and values affect you and your behavior.

Our attitude acts like a set of lenses through which we see the world around us. How are yours tinted or tainted? Do you see the world through rose-colored lenses? Or, are yours blue? Does life look bright or appear dull? Do you see the glass as half full or half empty? Are you an optimist, a pessimist, or a realist? Do you see opportunities or problems? We answer such questions to understand and accept our attitude.

Webster's New World Dictionary defines attitude as "a manner of acting, feeling, or thinking that shows one's disposition, opinion, mental set, etc." One's "mental set" strikes the most resonant chord for me. We've looked at the components of our mental set by examining our core beliefs and values. And these beliefs and values held deeply in place within us determine our disposition, mental set, perspective, and even our body language. With further examination we can begin to see what makes up, our attitude.

We've all likely heard someone say, "You need to change your attitude," or "That's not the attitude we want people to have around here". But, changing your attitude is not so simple. However, when we become aware of and understand what contributes to our attitude, we can shift it to one that serves us more effectively.

Someone once asked me, "Where did you get such a positive attitude?" The answer: I've come to know and to accept that I also have a very strong negative side that I can just as easily choose. I don't like feeling negative, so I choose to be more positive and to focus on the opportunities in front of me. When I held the core belief that "I'm not enough," with its corresponding values of excellence, productivity, success, and competition, my attitude expressed "win" or "lose." I saw situations in life as competitions: "I must win. I must be the best. I must be perfect." Perfection sets us up for dissatisfaction. With my new belief that "I'm enough," my values shifted to integrity, balance, peace of mind, love, helping others, self-expression, and relationships; my attitude in turn shifted to "win-win." It continues to evolve into an attitude of gratitude. As cliché as that may sound, I am more and more grateful for what I have, rather than focusing on all that I don't have.

Again, we can change an aspect of ourselves that relates to an organized structure deep within us. Using the Internal Operating System model, we can access our own structure at any one of these stages. And when we create a change at any level, the other levels will shift in both directions. This allows us to do the work with ourselves at the level we are conscious of and does not preclude anyone from making sustainable behavior changes—even simple efforts of "behavior modification."

Having taught tennis, film acting, executive presentation skills, communication skills, and team-building, I've learned that a newly acquired behavior doesn't usually "stick" if nothing else within the internal structure has changed. If all that changes is the behavior itself, at some point under stress or duress, the old habit will return.

"Pessimism never won any battle."

—Dwight D. Eisenhower

CHAPTER 5

THOUGHTS AND FEELINGS

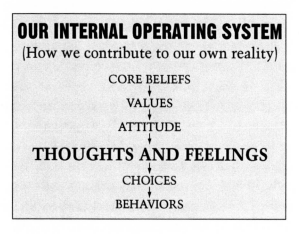

OUR INTERNAL OPERATING SYSTEM
(How we contribute to our own reality)

CORE BELIEFS
↓
VALUES
↓
ATTITUDE
↓
THOUGHTS AND FEELINGS
↓
CHOICES
↓
BEHAVIORS

"Thought is God's gift to you; what you think about is your gift to yourself."

—Prem Rawat

Our thoughts and feelings provide us with a guidance system: nature's way of giving us direction through our logic and our emotions—from our head and from our heart. Along the lines of "you are what you think," years ago some wonderful corporate training colleagues shared this maxim from Stephen Covey's *Seven Habits of Highly Effective People*. It continues to remind me how I contribute to my reality:

Sow a thought	*reap an action,*
Sow an action	*reap a habit,*
Sow a habit	*reap a character,*
Sow a character	*reap a destiny.*

Words are powerful. Thoughts are powerful. Words have the power to influence others to action. The average person speaks about 125 words per minute (wpm). Some of us speak more quickly, others more slowly. Some cultures speak faster; some speak slower. Even when we speak extemporaneously, we edit what we say, as we know how powerful our words can be. We think (or talk to ourselves) four to six times faster than we speak which implies that when we talk to ourselves, we don't edit. We say things to ourselves that we would never say out loud. Some things we say to ourselves are questionable, some untrue, and some are negative. If words have the power to influence others to action, imagine the influence we have over ourselves. We spend considerable time intentionally trying to influence others yet how conscious are we of influencing ourselves? We, in fact, regularly influence ourselves by what we tell ourselves. Of all of the people that we influence, we have the greatest influence on ourselves. Our thoughts and feelings constantly influence our actions.

SELF-TALK

Life is a conversation! We're having a conversation with ourselves much of the time. What we say to ourselves has a profound effect on our behavior. *Self-talk* is this conversation inside our heads. This inner conversation can lead us to discover who we are and how we operate.

When you listen to your thoughts, do you notice any repetitive patterns? Is the voice inside your head supportive or critical? Is it riddled with fear and doubt? Is it your saboteur or your best friend? The following short story offers you an inspiring example of how to use your self-talk to create desirable behaviors:

At the 1988 Summer Olympics in Seoul, Korea, a young American diver named Greg Louganis dove for the Gold Medal on the ten-meter platform. On his next-to-last dive, in a very dramatic moment, he hit his head on the platform during a very difficult reverse maneuver before his out-of-control body hit the water. Clearly hurt, he was helped out of the water and, moving slowly, escorted into the locker room. The world watched not knowing how serious his injury was. Milking the moment for all it was worth, the TV announcers reminded the audience about "the agony and the ecstasy". They went on to say that if Louganis was fit to, he now needed a 9.8, a near perfect dive, to win the Gold Medal. His competition, Xiong Ni, a sixteen-year-old boy from the Peoples Republic of China, had already finished his complete routine and now stood in first place. A major upset appeared in the making. After a long ten minutes or so, Louganis emerged from the locker room, his head in bandages, ready to dive his final dive.

Louganis approached the ladder very slowly, climbed up to the platform, set himself and executed his dive— 9.8—to win the Gold Medal! The crowd went wild. (This is why I love sports so much. It's high drama! You never quite know what will happen until the final moment.) Louganis exited the pool, and one of the American announcers immediately approached him with a microphone and asked, "So Greg, what was going on in your mind knowing that you needed an almost perfect dive, knowing that your young competitor was in first place, and knowing that you just cracked your head open on your last dive?" (At this moment, I realized we were about to hear the champion's *self-talk*.) Louganis looked at the announcer and calmly answered, "Well, as I was coming out of the locker room and approaching the ladder, I told myself three things: First, I said to myself, 'Greg, you've been here before. You know what this pressure is about. You've won two Gold medals four years ago in Los Angeles. Secondly, you've practiced this dive every day for the last four years…just do what you do in practice… just let go. And thirdly, what's the worst thing that will happen if I don't get a 9.8? I'll be considered the second best diver in the entire world, and my mother will still love me anyway.'"

This athlete not only trained physically to Olympic standards but also trained mentally to relax himself and to create the behaviors necessary to excel and to win. He chose to influence himself in a realistic way, and his *self-talk* supported his desired outcome. If you look at the top ten male or female tennis players or golfers in the world, any one of them can beat any of the other ones, on any given day. They all have technique and talent; that's what puts them into the top ten category. What separates the champions from the rest? What is it that contributes to those number one players staying at that level? It's their mental game that continually gives them the edge over the rest of their opponents.

Though this rare and dramatic story of Louganis winning exemplifies how our thoughts and feelings affect our behavior, ordinary people's *self-talk* perpetually influences their daily actions, as well. When we attend a major meeting; stand up to give a presentation in front of a large audience; approach an important conversation with our mate, partner, or friend; or take on an important task, our thoughts and feelings usually precede our behavior.

For example, I recently conducted presentation skills training programs for IBM executives in Bangalore, India. I held five days of trainings with a different group each day. On the third day, I came down to the hotel lobby to wait for my 7:45 AM taxi as I had done each of the other two mornings. I needed plenty of time to get across town in Bangalore, but 7:45 AM came and went with no driver arriving for me. A steady stream of people exited the elevators and got into their taxis, but I still waited. I noticed that I had begun to pace back and forth in the lobby, and I was even getting angry. I began to tell myself, "I hate to be late. This is very unprofessional. IBM is paying me a lot money to run these programs, and I'm going to be late." Then I heard my judgmental voice say, "How could they call this the Silicon Valley of India? The infrastructure here is horrible. When are they going to get professional taxi drivers instead of these people?" I had worked myself into a very angry and uptight state. Then I became aware of how stressed I was. I took a very deep breath and asked myself, "What else is true for me right now?" I told myself, "Well, even if I am late, they can't begin the course without me. They will read their emails and look at their phones to pass the time until I arrive. And, wait a minute, I'm in India! What a wonderful life that I get to work in so many different and interesting parts of the world." As I calmed down, I asked myself, "What else can I do right now to influence this situation?" I turned toward the front desk, walked over to the concierge (I don't know why I didn't do this before), and asked him if the hotel had a car that could take me to IBM. He replied, "Yes, sir." He arranged the car immediately, and I actually arrived fifteen minutes earlier than any of the participants.

I have practiced the *self-talk* technique for many, many years, and it remains a solidly reliable tool for the countless stressful situations that I experience in my life. By looking at a situation differently, I can change my state of mind and my state of being.

Remember the formula that I mentioned earlier, *Performance = Potential - Self Interference?* Consider all of the ways that we "self-interfere". We worry, doubt ourselves, criticize ourselves, judge ourselves, judge others, try too hard, don't try hard enough, and praise ourselves. Yes, even self-praise can become a form of interference.

I remember years ago being on a tennis court and hitting a beautiful down-the-line forehand shot. It felt perfect. And just as I said to myself, "That was incredible. You just hit such a wonderful shot," the ball came back faster than I had hit it. Now I was no longer in the right place to return it and hit it into the net. I was no longer present. I was reviewing how wonderful the past moment had been and lost the present moment. When we become aware of and limit such "self-interference," we can increase our performance. When we choose to pay attention we can access ourselves through our thoughts and feelings. The payoff can be plentiful when we learn how to "get out of our own way."

EXERCISE: SELF-TALK

Use the blank diagram, Figure 1, as you follow the directions below. Refer to the completed diagram, Figure 1A, as a guideline while reflecting upon your own self-talk.

Self-Talk Diagram

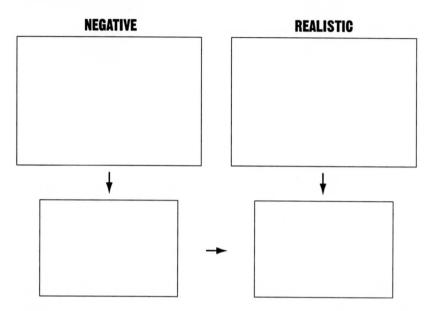

Figure 1

1. Choose something in your life that you feel required to do, whether at work or at home. Draw two boxes side by side. In the left-hand box, write down some of the *negative* thoughts and statements that you have about this particular activity, such as, "Why do I have to do this?" "I am not very good at this." "This is not what I expected when I agreed to this." "I hate this." "I hope I don't screw up." "I'm going to be judged."

2. After writing down some of your favorite negative, less supportive, thoughts, in the space below the box, identify how you would actually appear when you have these thoughts. List some of your likely behaviors under such

circumstances, such as "defensive," "tight," "overly cautious," "fumbling," "angry," "withdrawn," and so on.

3. Now move to the right side and below the right-hand box list your desired behaviors. Ideally, how would you like to behave during this activity? "Calm," "knowledgeable," "professional," "open," "confident," "humorous," "available," and so on.

4. Considering that our thoughts affect our feelings and both contribute to our behavior, now move up into the right-hand box and write down some *realistic* thoughts and statements that you may say to yourself that would contribute to the ideal behaviors that you've listed below the box. Only write down those *realistic* things that ring true for you, such as, "I'm prepared." "I've done this before." "I know how to do this." "This is an opportunity for me to learn something about myself." "This needs to be done, and I have the skill to do it."

Sometimes we want to go from the negative to the positive, however, if you don't believe the statement you tell yourself, you will dismiss it as untrue, and it will have no affect on you. The key is, like Greg Louganis, to contribute to the conversation in a realistic way. He told himself things that rang true for him though they weren't necessarily "positive".

Here is an example of a client of mine, Figure 1A, who had to prepare to give an important presentation in front of his leadership team. Notice the process he went through from his initial negative self-talk to his realistic self-talk. As you look at this example, reflect upon your own process.

Self-Talk Diagram (sample)

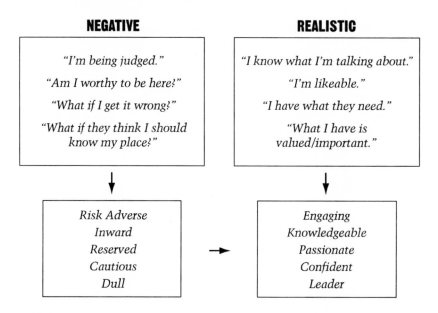

NEGATIVE	REALISTIC
"I'm being judged." *"Am I worthy to be here?"* *"What if I get it wrong?"* *"What if they think I should know my place?"*	*"I know what I'm talking about."* *"I'm likeable."* *"I have what they need."* *"What I have is valued/important."*
Risk Adverse *Inward* *Reserved* *Cautious* *Dull*	*Engaging* *Knowledgeable* *Passionate* *Confident* *Leader*

Figure 1A

Follow these guidelines to change your self-talk:

1. **Practice Awareness:** Become aware of your internal conversation prior to and during your task.

2. **Try To Understand:** Where are your *self-talk* thoughts coming from? Do they belong to a younger, less secure part of your self? Or, do they come from a judgmental part of your adult self?

3. **Encourage Improvement:** Add to your conversation. Tell yourself what is also true for you in this moment.

4. **Practice Reinforcement:** Practice with feedback brings improvement. Practice doesn't make perfect;

practice makes habits. Practice saying such supportive thoughts to yourself. Notice how you feel after saying these thoughts and notice the response within yourself from the result of a given task as well as the response from others.

Remember my original core belief that "I am not enough"? I discovered that belief by tuning in and listening to my self-talk and by noticing the patterns. No matter what I accomplished or how many compliments I received, I always heard that voice in my head, saying things like, "I could have done better." "They don't know it, but I left something out." "Uh, oh, now they may ask me to do this again. Now I have set myself up for failure."

Since working with my core beliefs, my inner conversation sounds more like, "This is an opportunity for me to grow." "I'm prepared." "I'm ready to give my best." "This is important and needs to be done." "I have good skills and can do what they ask of me." These new thoughts and feelings have allowed me to develop a greater sense of self-confidence and self-esteem.

When revisiting our internal system with greater awareness of how our thoughts and feelings affect our behavior, we can now self-manage. Few people regularly think about their core beliefs, values or attitude, though most of us know what we think or feel in a given moment. These thoughts and feelings give us ready access to our internal operating system, allowing us to affect change in both the direction of our behaviors as well as in the direction of our beliefs.

"Individuality is found in feelings."

—William James

CHAPTER 6

CHOICES

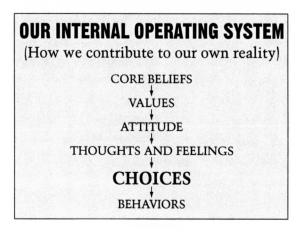

OUR INTERNAL OPERATING SYSTEM
(How we contribute to our own reality)

CORE BELIEFS
↓
VALUES
↓
ATTITUDE
↓
THOUGHTS AND FEELINGS
↓
CHOICES
↓
BEHAVIORS

*"Do not let what you cannot do interfere
with what you can do."*

—John Wooden

When I taught film acting classes in Los Angeles, actors talked a lot about choices. They commonly asked, "What are my choices?" "What choices should I make as this character?" Actors who worked from the inside out asked themselves questions like, "In what situation does the character find himself?" "What does the character believe to be true about herself?" "What does she value?" "What's his attitude?" "What does the character think and feel in this situation?" By examining the character's internal life, the choices and behaviors become apparent. This excellent example of how an actor builds a character illustrates how one's internal life creates his or her choices and behaviors.

Happiness is a choice. Unhappiness is a choice. To shift is a choice. Behavior change is about choice. We make choices continuously—some of them consciously, some of them unconsciously, that is, based on our need to survive (or at least to save face). Unconscious choices don't feel like choices at all; they feel and appear more like reactions. We must face the fact that at times, we don't want to take responsibility for the outcome of our behavior and ultimately for our lives. People commonly say, "What do you mean it was my choice? I just reacted." A reaction, or "knee jerk response," expresses an unconscious choice.

Let's focus on the empowering quality of *conscious choice.* Choice gives us freedom to create, and yet every choice carries a trade-off or consequence. Our logic and our emotions, our head and our heart, constantly inform us how we think or feel in any given moment, thus offering us choices of how to behave. When we make a choice, it becomes a decision and ultimately manifests as our behavior. Choosing not to make a decision also expresses a choice, implying that we choose to be a victim. In Victor Frankl's book, *Man's Search for Meaning*, he questions the truth of the theory that human beings are mere products of biological, psychological, and social factors. He writes:

> *"We who lived in concentration camps can remember the men who walked through the huts comforting others, giving their last piece of bread. They may have been few in number, but they offer sufficient proof that everything can be taken from a man but one thing: the last of the human freedoms—*

to choose one's attitude in any given set of circumstances, to choose one's own way. And there were always choices to make. Every day, every hour, offered the opportunity to make a decision, a decision which determined whether you would or would not submit to those powers which threatened to rob you of your very self, your inner freedom, which determined whether or not you would become the plaything of circumstance, renouncing freedom and dignity to become molded into the form of the typical inmate."

With this concept beautifully expressed through Frankl's eyes, I'm inspired to apply his premise to working in the corporate world or being in a relationship. When someone asks something of us or we feel something "done to us," we may choose how to respond to such a request from another or to an action taken against us. There's no need or value in choosing to be victims. We can choose to stay or choose to go. We can choose to speak up or choose to remain quiet. We can choose to agree or choose to disagree. We always have a choice.

Strongly fearing failure, my original core belief: "I am not enough," caused me to be very cautious about whether or not to participate in presented situations. With my new belief: "I am enough," I now regularly choose to participate in what life offers me because failure no longer threatens me. I now choose to learn from each experience.

In the training, consulting, and coaching world we often refer to "our sphere of influence vs. our sphere of concerns". Stephen Covey illustrates this concept quite well in *The Seven Habits of Highly Effective People*. A myriad of circumstances in both our immediate and not so immediate environment affect us, yet we all too often feel helpless to influence them. The global economy, the war on terrorism, poverty, disease in Third World countries, global warming, decisions made by our governments, and so on, concern many people. And, sometimes we feel victimized, worrying and complaining about circumstances out of our control. Simultaneously we directly impact certain situations well within our control. Our community, our customers, our employees, our young children, our partners (to some degree), and the person that we have the most control over—our self—all fall within our sphere of influence. In addition, every time that we exercise this sphere of influence, our sphere expands and ripples out into our larger sphere of concerns.

In essence, this book attempts to emphasize that the individual that we can most influence is our self. The next time that you become aware of your worrying and complaining about things out of your control that you cannot influence, like the decision just made by your CEO, or your company's Board of Directors, or the President of the United States, or even the weather, stop for a moment. Make a different choice and redirect your energy toward what you can definitely change: yourself.

Happiness is a choice; it doesn't just happen. Unhappiness is a choice. Peace is a choice. We choose. Our world overflows with positive and negative experiences. We can look at the glass as half full or half empty. We can look at it as if it's completely full. It remains our choice. The situation is what it is. As we used to say when I taught tennis: "The ball is where it is." We have no control over where the oncoming ball is, but we do have choice over where we are in relationship to it. Do you want to be close … or far from it? As you view your life situations, how do you want to respond to them? You can choose. What choices are you making? If you are not experiencing what you say you want to experience, why aren't you? What are you choosing in this moment?

"I believe that we are solely responsible for our choices, and we have to accept the consequences of every deed, word, and thought throughout our lifetime."

—Elizabeth Kubler-Ross

CHAPTER 7

BEHAVIORS

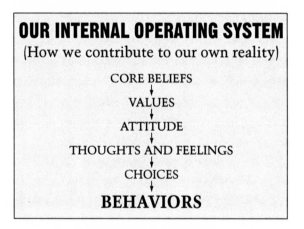

OUR INTERNAL OPERATING SYSTEM
(How we contribute to our own reality)

CORE BELIEFS
↓
VALUES
↓
ATTITUDE
↓
THOUGHTS AND FEELINGS
↓
CHOICES
↓
BEHAVIORS

"What you do speaks so loudly,
that I can't hear what you're saying."

—Ralph Waldo Emerson

You probably bought this book for the contents of this chapter, and you may have even skimmed the other chapters first to discover if I have something new to say about changing your behavior. Actually, if you haven't yet learned from the previous chapters how you contribute to your own reality, how you, in fact, create your own behavior, then this chapter probably won't be much help to you.

Having said that, this chapter intends to offer you additional tools and skills that will support your desire to change behavior that no longer works for you.

We constantly interact, react, and engage with our partners, our bosses, our employees, and our children. We don't live in a vacuum. We are continually in relationship. For me, writing this book was like entering into a new relationship. And, the decision to write it presented me with a major choice in my life, and this choice required certain behaviors and changes. I had to further explore my beliefs, my values, and my thoughts and feelings, in order to write about a subject that holds great meaning for me. And, I want to share some of that process of making real change in my behavior.

Having been a coach, and workshop leader for over 30 years, I decided to try my hand at writing for the first time. Through this invaluable process I revisited some old beliefs and behaviors. For instance, though this chapter nears the end of this book, I have much more information that I want to share with you, and yet I'm keenly aware of possibly overwhelming you as I have been when reading some books. When I asked for feedback from the people in my life that I respect and love, they encouraged me to make it real, not to worry about making it right. Being task-oriented, my old underlying belief of "not being good enough" called me to look again at my intention for this book: to help others understand more about themselves and how to approach real change in their behavior through self-reflection and honest action. And to that end, my sharing continues.

REFLECTION AND EXPRESSION

Here we are at the output stage of our internal operating system. In previous chapters, we have looked at, discussed, and reflected upon the internal part of our operating system. Our behavior is our expression. It's expressed outwardly; it's our *output*, what's literally seen and heard, not what others infer or interpret our behavior to be. I have had the privilege to coach many senior executives around the world in regard to their behavior when speaking to and leading others. It fascinates me to see how they express themselves in their roles as leaders. Each of them, in their expression, reflects the world they live in and who they believe themselves to be. Their core beliefs and values come shining through. We all express and reflect who we believe ourselves to be. With that in mind, let me share some key elements of Body Language that will help you be more aware of how you express yourself through your observable behavior.

BODY LANGUAGE

When I'm introduced to a new client or to a new group of participants in a workshop, I'm fascinated by how each individual walks and talks, stands and sits, makes eye contact, and how much space each requires when meeting others. By observing them from the outside in, I begin to learn how each person may be thinking, feeling, and, making choices as they participate. My observation leads to my perception and that perception becomes my reality.

To a great extent, life is about managing perception. How well are you managing perceptions in your life? How do people receive and discern the messages of your body language? Are your messages consistent or do you send mixed messages? Your body's language, the message *and* the delivery of it, has three key components: Visual, Vocal, and Verbal. Dr. Albert Mehrabian, UCLA Professor Emeritus, has offered these statistics to emphasize that our body speaks louder than our words. Our body language expresses itself as:

55% Visual (our stance, posture, gestures, movement, eye contact, etc.)

38% Vocal (our volume, rate of speech, inflections, modulation, pauses, etc.)

7% Verbal (the actual words we use when speaking)

As a communicator, facilitator, and teacher of communication, when I first saw these statistics, I thought, "This can't be. You mean to tell me that words aren't important?" To the contrary, I had come to know that words are very important. However, if your body language does not reflect your words, those words become the secondary message. How many times have we heard the sayings, "Actions speak louder than words," "Practice what you preach" or, "Walk your talk"? Our body language makes such an impact that it sends a louder message than our words.

As you explore your internal operating system you can make changes at any of the different stages. When you make a change it will affect your inner environment in both directions. For example, if you change your self-talk to be more realistic or even positive, not only will it present you with new choices, it will also affect what you believe about yourself and the situation you are facing. This chapter intends to focus your changes at the behavior level.

When I began running workshops in communication skills, I received feedback that when I didn't smile, I came across as intense and people felt reluctant to approach me. This feedback stunned me since I internally experience myself as very approachable and easy-going. However, I accept that all feedback carries some degree of truth. So, I decided to see for myself by videotaping myself in front of a group. I saw firsthand what they were referring to, and I then understood why people didn't approach me on the coffee breaks. With that awareness and understanding, I made more of an effort to smile and to relax my face when I was speaking. The result was that by contributing to a different perception, I got a different result. People began to gather around me during coffee breaks and wanted to know more. This new behavior did not integrate immediately. In order for this to become my new way of communicating, I had to go through the stages of creating lasting change that we've looked at a number of times throughout this book.

• Feedback from people and the video provided the **Awareness.**

• **Understanding** came from recognizing my need to be significant and not taken lightly.

• **Improvement** came from simply making a new choice and by relaxing my face.

• **Reinforcement** came from experiencing the participants' reaction and feeling my impact on them.

OBSERVABLE BEHAVIOR

Observable behavior means the outward behavior that we can see or hear (like a video camera would see and hear), *not* what we infer. For example, we see someone scowl, look upward, and scratch his head. If we ask a group what they saw, their invariable response will be something like: "We saw his confusion or indecision; he seemed to be looking for something; he looked upset." These are not observations but rather inferences or interpretations.

Let's now look at the different types of behavior that we exhibit and how our thinking patterns affect those behaviors. To reiterate: our beliefs affect our values that in turn influence our attitude that affects our thoughts and feelings. We're then presented with choices, which when chosen and acted upon, appear as our behavior. No mystery. It's as simple as that—but also hard work.

Having given many individuals in corporate work teams the opportunity to spend a couple of days observing and reflecting upon their internal operating system, I have found that many of us may share similar beliefs, and even have many values in common. Yet we behave quite differently from each other. We have different personalities. We go about our tasks differently, we use meetings differently, we problem solve differently, and we communicate differently. Two of my clients, for example, who have been working together for over ten years recently each completed the Values Review and Clarification Exercise (see page 22) and discovered that they share seven out of their top ten values, and yet they display very different behavioral styles. One is very task-oriented, and the other is very people-oriented. One is focused on results, the other on a vision. Why is it that much of the time their observable behavior—visually, vocally, and verbally— differs from each other? They think about tasks differently and then approach them differently. Sometimes they disagree strongly enough that they experience conflict between them. If such a conflict doesn't reach deep into core beliefs and values, then the conflict is usually style-based.

I initially trained in behavioral modeling with the authors of *Social Style/Management Style*, Dorothy and Robert

Bolton. Two industrial psychologists, David W. Merrill and Roger H. Reid, originally developed the SOCIAL STYLES* model. Their book, *Personal Styles and Effective Performance* explains the four-quadrant model of personal styles. In the early 1960s, Merrill and Reid had the opportunity to develop an assessment tool for determining an individual's suitability for a particular role or job description. The tool was an attempt to see if certain behaviors could predict success in leadership, management, and sales careers. For example, if decision-making is required, what type of personal Style can best perform this skill? If ideas need generating, what type of personal Style would best fit this? If support is needed, what type of personal Style suits this? If finance and operations need managing, what's the best type of person for this skill?

Ironically, using such questions, they found that the model wasn't successful in determining what type of person would be best suited for a particular role. However, they *did* discover a practical, easy-to-understand model for managing and improving interpersonal relationships.

ASSERTIVENESS AND RESPONSIVENESS

Most of our observable behaviors can be grouped into two dimensions: *assertiveness* and *responsiveness*. The assertive dimension refers to the forcefulness or directedness of our behaviors. Do you tend to tell or ask others in order to get your needs met? Do you speak more quickly and loudly, or more slowly and softly? The responsive dimension refers to how much emotion you display in your behaviors. Do you control your emotions or do you show others what you are feeling?

BEHAVIORAL STYLES

The behavioral model presented here reveals not how we see ourselves but how others *literally* see or hear us, based on their perception.

The following SOCIAL STYLES behavioral model (Figure 2) introduces the different types of behaviors that we display in our lives—to others—in both work and play on a daily basis.

Four-Quadrant Behavioral Model

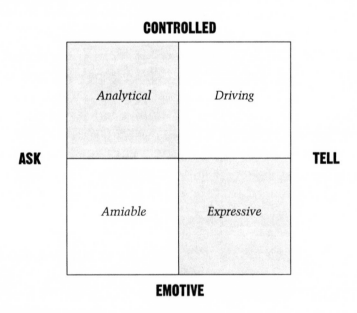

Figure 2

This two-dimensional grid shows us four distinctive behavioral Styles. All people exhibit all four Styles at one time or another; however, in most situations others perceive an individual to exhibit a dominant Style. The four distinct Styles are as follows:

1. The **Driving Style** displays the assertive but emotionally controlled style: task-oriented, time-oriented, results-oriented, resonates with the bottom line.

2. The **Expressive Style** exhibits an assertive but emotionally responsive style: spontaneous, enthusiastic, people-oriented, fun-loving, sees the big picture.

3. The **Amiable Style** expresses the less assertive but emotionally responsive style: supportive, team-oriented, people-oriented, cooperative, seeks harmony.

4. The **Analytical Style** displays the less assertive but emotionally controlled style: task-oriented, process-oriented, factual, detailed, wants precision.

FLEXIBILITY

I have learned from working with this model that no Style is better than another. Each is simply different. There's no better place on the grid. Success can come from any Style. However, understanding the differences can make for more effective interactions with others. Rather than putting each other into boxes, we can learn to build bridges to each other. This behavioral skill is called *Versatility*, and it is the key to benefiting from this type of behavioral model. Behavior change just for the sake of change has no meaning, but advocating change for the sake of improved relations with others results in greater success. We can accomplish this by making some different choices and modifying some of our behaviors. It's not about changing our personality. Success can be improved when we access the strengths of the other Styles. By accessing the strengths of another Style we can meet that person "where they live." This fosters greater rapport, and rapport must be established to create good communication. Otherwise, we are simply talking *at* each other rather than *to* each other.

We are all familiar with The Golden Rule: "Do unto others as you would have them do unto you" or in modern terms: "Treat others the way you want to be treated." And, how do most people want to be treated? People want to be treated with fairness, with respect, and with honesty. If you behave in this manner, people see you as a flexible person with integrity. Dr. Tony Alessandra has been credited with the concept of the Platinum Rule: "Treat others the way they want to be treated."

For example, an analytical person wants to be treated differently than an expressive person. The Analytical Style wants the facts, the details, the background. The Expressive Style wants to know how a situation will serve their individual needs, their team's needs, and their organization's needs. When interacting with others the Amiable Style wants to feel that the relationship is intact, that harmony will be maintained. The Driving Style wants to know the bottom line, what's necessary to get the task done. No better or worse, just different. The more we can be flexible in adapting our behaviors to other personalities and situations, the more success we can experience.

Throughout this book, I've shared the example of how I shifted a core belief ("I am not enough") and how that shift ("I am enough") affected my values, attitude, thoughts and feelings, and choices. My personality has been profiled as a Driving Style. For as long as I can remember, I have been strongly oriented toward producing results; I focus on the bottom line and cut to the chase; mine is a time-oriented style. Even though I changed a specific core belief that affected my values, attitude, thoughts and feelings, and choices—which have all changed—my essential behavioral style remains the same. The change I made allowed me to access the strengths of the other three Styles and become more flexible and more versatile—all of which enable me to work with many different types of personalities with successful results. For instance, when I chose to write this book, I had to remind myself all throughout the process that my readers would have a variety of Styles rather than always be like my own. Initially, I would have been most comfortable writing from only my task-oriented, result-oriented Style, leaving out the personal touch. Instead I chose a flexible and more open approach to hopefully resonate with all Styles.

CREATING LASTING CHANGE

Whether you want to change your core beliefs, your inner voice, your golf swing, the way you manage your time and activities in the office, how you adapt to a person with a different style than yours, or any specific behavior, these four principles offer you the steps necessary to create lasting behavior change in your life.

Awareness and acceptance are the first steps to creating lasting change.

Understanding what holds habitual behavior in place is key to doing things differently.

Improvement means making a new choice and replacing old behavior patterns with more effective and productive ones.

Reinforcement emphasizes that practice with feedback brings improvement.

* * *

My hope and intention in writing this book has been to help you understand the things that contribute to your behaviors and how they affect your life. I don't want to imply that changing our behavior is always easy. It can be hard work, and the choice to change requires constant vigilance and recognition of our old modes. Discipline is something to be valued. Freedom comes from discipline. By having a clear intention of what you want to create and how you would like to be, and then applying the discipline to do what's necessary, you can experience a newfound freedom in your life.

"Well done is better than well said."

—Ben Franklin

FINAL THOUGHTS

"One does not become enlightened by imagining figures of light, but by making the darkness conscious."

—Carl G. Jung

We cannot create real effective change in our lives if we choose to simply chase after our own tail *figuratively speaking*. So what is it that we *literally* chase? Why do we continue to behave the way we do, even when we want to change? The truth is: we change only when we come to understand and accept who we truly are—then, shift happens.

SHIFT HAPPENS!

When shift happens, our behavior integrates into our internal operating system. Shift happens naturally when we least expect it. We have an experience and then we enter into a change process. We *think* about what just happened. Some of us actually *feel* what just happened. Shift is dynamic not static. But shift takes time. Sometimes we go through an extended change process, as William Bridges points out in his book *Transitions*. Endings happen. We lose a loved one. Our boss has been promoted. We're let go from a job. A relationship ends. An ending begins a transition. New beginnings also happen. We meet someone new and exciting. A child is born and comes into our life. We get promoted. How do we deal with these familiar changes? Too often we judge them as good or bad rather than effective and less effective. Rumi, the 13th century Persian poet, said, "Out beyond ideas of right-doing and wrong-doing, there is a field. I'll meet you there". Judgment stops the process cold. If we examine our internal structure with judgment, we get stuck. There's no movement. There's no flow. We dampen our creativity and, in severe cases, we shut down.

Note: In *The Artist's Way*, Julia Cameron offers her "morning pages" process (writing three pages each morning) to bring our "self-talk" to the surface—out and gone. Such a practice keeps us current, clears away our inner noise, gets us unstuck, and allows us to enjoy the moment.

Bridge's work points out that the transitions between endings and new beginnings make this life a journey. Endings and New Beginnings represent destinations and places; the Neutral Zone in between opens to the journey where we can experiment with life using trial and error. We can explore new ways of seeing, new ways of thinking, and new ways of behaving.

After many years of self-exploration, I allowed myself to open to the power of "surrender," to not knowing. Becoming comfortable with this "not knowing" is the challenge. Human nature wants to know. A brilliant acting teacher of mine once shared, "Knowing is death; not knowing is aliveness." When we think we know, we stop looking and listening. When we acknowledge that we really don't know, our senses come alive, and we enter the present. Most of us experience great discomfort in "not knowing," so we keep busy. We keep moving. We keep running. We keep doing. We become human doings, rather than human beings. Interrupt the speed! The slowing down, remembering what is real, introduces us to ourselves and to our environment. A key to learning how to feel comfortable with "not knowing," lies in the simplicity of our breath.

PRESENCE

The breath has no past and has no future. It simply comes and goes. It's always present as long as we are alive. This opens us to our own presence, and we need this presence to examine our internal operating system. Remember wherever we put our attention, that's where we are. By placing our attention on our breath, we practice presence.

Back to the computer analogy that I began with: No matter whether you use Mac OS, Windows, or Linux as your operating system, you still must be plugged into a power source. (Remember, you as a person have a system, you have a program running on that system, and ultimately, you are the programmer.)

Our internal operating system too, must be powered by some source. This power resides in the breath. Without it, our internal operating system doesn't work. Each breath gives us the gift of life. We take well over fifteen thousand breaths during our waking hours each day. (Notice how many breaths that you are aware of. Improvement, not perfection!) Breathing reminds us that our life is not static but dynamic. It offers us the ultimate metaphor of the ebb and flow. It allows us to let go. It comes in and it goes out. By forming a relationship with our breath, we can let go of what no longer serves us. There is nothing to do. We open to the experience of being. Simply being. I am, you are, we are … being breathed.

As you examine your own operating system, heighten your awareness as you discover your beliefs. Notice your values shifting within their grouping. Witness your attitude being tinted or tainted a different color than it was a few moments ago. Listen to your *self-talk*. Listen to your gut and notice what you feel. Choice empowers us. Participate in deciding your life's direction—when you choose to choose, or when you choose not to. And, finally, be conscious of your actions as they are manifesting your internal process. Allow your breath to teach you how to live life moment by moment, one breath at a time.

The Scottish psychiatrist, R. D. Laing, poetically describes the denial reflex: "The range of what we think and do is limited by what we fail to notice. And because we fail to notice that we're failing to notice, there is little that we can do to change, until we notice how failing to notice, shapes our thoughts and deeds."

Become your own observer; observe your own becoming. Become an adaptive human being, a learning being.

*"To look is one thing,
To see what you look at is another,
To understand what you see is a third,
To learn from what you understand
is something else,
But to act on what you learn
is all that really matters. "*

—Anonymous

RECOMMENDED READING

The Road Less Traveled **by Scott Peck**

Mastery **by George Leonard**

The Inner Game of Tennis **by Timothy Gallwey**

The Wisdom of No Escape **by Pema Chodron**

Creative Visualization **by Shakti Gawain**

The Artist's Way **by Julia Cameron**

ADDITIONAL TOOLS FOR YOUR TOOL BELT

It's been a fascinating journey writing this book and hopefully my journey of learning and growing will go on as I continue to write, coach, and teach. It has always been my intention to help my self and others to discover how to move through this life with greater ease. I well remember what Scott Peck said in the first line of his book, *The Road Less Traveled*: "Life is difficult." In this spirit, I want to share with you some additional tools and skills to add to your tool belt. As I like to remind my workshop participants, if all you have is a hammer, the whole world looks like a nail. Behavior change is experiential. You can't learn it from a book. I highly recommend that you take this book and find an experiential workshop, a good life coach or executive coach to work with you one-on-one. Whether you choose to change a core belief that you hold, or change your inner dialogue, or adapt to another style of behaving, here are some additional tools for you.

STAGES OF SKILL BUILDING

When we learn a new skill or behavior we can expect to experience predictable stages of skill building. Whether we're learning a new golf grip, or "active listening," or how to reach working agreements with others, it helps immensely to understand how we learn. Even though we have different learning styles, just like we have different behavioral styles, we usually begin with an unconscious incompetence and build to an unconscious competence as the four stages reveal below:

Unconscious Incompetence

At this initial stage of openness and naiveté, we don't even know what we don't know. This is the new beginner. Usually eager and optimistic, we don't know what the task involves. I remember beginning the process of writing this book, thinking, this isn't difficult, lots of people write books. I was the true beginner. I didn't know what it would take.

Conscious Incompetence

At this humbling stage of skill building, we discover what's required, and we know what we don't know. We recognize the work, effort, and practice involved. (This may be the most important stage of learning, as we identify what we need to do in order to learn the new skill.) At this stage, some people may decide that they cannot accomplish what they had originally intended. This stage benefits from being coached. At this stage when I began to write, I realized that it required certain skills, discipline and knowledge that I wasn't sure I had. I realized and appreciated how difficult writing really is.

Conscious Competence

Now we know what we know. We can perform the new skill, though we do it consciously with required concentration and effort. With practice, with guidance from my skilled editor, with help from other authors that I knew, I began to craft this book with a newfound confidence, while remaining conscious of what I needed to learn.

Unconscious Competence

At this integrated stage we don't even think about what we know, like the Nike ad says: You just do it. As in making love, driving a car, and riding a bicycle, the new skill becomes second nature. For example, many professional athletes operate at this stage, and yet very few can teach or coach others to do the same. As a new writer, I'm not sure that I have arrived at this integrated stage, though I very much look forward to writing another book with less effort and more ease.

During the stages of Conscious Incompetence where a lot of effort is required, developing the skill of relaxed concentration is an invaluable tool. Coaching can help with this very important step. Tim Gallwey, in his *Inner Game* books, focuses on this skill as fundamental to learning.

RELAXED CONCENTRATION

Whether you want to change a behavior, or change your self-talk, or change a core belief, concentration and focus are required. Relaxed concentration can be approached through three stages: Discipline, Interest, and Absorption.

Discipline

Whenever we try something new, like joining a gym, or creating an exercise routine, or attempting a diet, or writing a book, it requires a lot of discipline. We need to constantly remind ourselves to focus, to pay attention, to stay committed. Many of us are not very disciplined and quite often, we lose our focus. For this reason, changing behavior can be frustrating at times, and we tend to give up. When I began to write and even throughout the process, I had to constantly set goals to accomplish the next task. I procrastinated and struggled much of the time. I can't tell you how many times I nearly gave up.

Interest

The key to sustaining concentration is to become interested in the new behavior or activity. Just like a great conversation or a good film, or reading an intriguing novel, we don't need to remind ourselves to concentrate when we are truly interested. Be curious. Become fascinated with your new behavior. Notice the nuances and intricacies of what you are attempting to do. This step has been critical for me as a writer, especially noticing when my writing flows, and when it's blocked. As I reconnect with my values and intention to help others' live their passion and enhance their communication, my writing opens up: I can say what I truly mean, and it flows more easily.

Absorption

This final stage calls for a very high state of concentration. When we become really interested in our new behavior, it absorbs us. When we least expect it, it begins to feel effortless. There is only the new behavior, as if we lose ourselves in the activity. We've then arrived at the "unconscious competent" stage of building a new skill or behavior. Athletes refer to this stage as being "in the zone". It's effortless effort. For instance, I vividly remember when paragraphs and sometimes a complete chapter of this book emerged from me, effortlessly and the feeling of joy that would accompany it.

MY INVITATION

I invite you to begin the process of behavior change and to explore using these skills and tools to the best of your ability. By practicing these stages of concentration when attempting to change a behavior, you will move through the phases of change in a more effortless manner resulting in a greater result. There are many wonderful coaches that can assist you in applying these skills, and others, to accomplish the success and fulfillment that you seek and deserve in your life. I wish you all the best.

NEXT STEPS

Now that you've been introduced to and understand your personal operating system, you may want to follow-this up with some training and/or coaching.

Feel free to contact us at **www.hankfieger.com**. We would be happy to discuss your personal needs, and your organizations needs, and offer some follow on sessions.

ABOUT THE AUTHOR

Hank Fieger is a professional observer of human behavior. He is President of Hank Fieger Associates, an international management consulting, training and coaching organization. He began his career in the training and development field in 1976, when he was trained as a coach by Timothy Gallwey, acclaimed author of *The Inner Game of Tennis*, helping him to develop a staff of trainers.

Hank has worked with many Fortune 100 and Fortune 500 companies in over 20 countries. His expertise is in Behavioral Executive Coaching, Team Building, Executive Presentation Skills, Personal Leadership and Leadership Communication Skills, using a model of open and honest communication. By combining his knowledge in both the fields of business and psychology, he found that he could help others in the required skills of "people management," and leadership. He especially enjoys working with executives who have strong technical or financial backgrounds.

Raised on Long Island, NY, he moved to California in 1970. In 1997 he relocated to Sydney, Australia working in Asia Pacific, and now enjoys much of his time working in Europe.

His dream is to help others reach their unique potential.

NOTES

NOTES

NOTES

NOTES

NOTES

NOTES

Printed in the United Kingdom by
Lightning Source UK Ltd., Milton Keynes
139891UK00001B/40/P